Instagram Marketing

Avdhesh Saxena

Introduction

Do you want to grow your Instagram following without spending a fortune?

No followers? No problem. This book will show you step-by-step techniques to grow your Instagram following, create an engaged audience, and generate leads.

You don't need millions of followers to grow your business. One thousand true fans is good enough.

Today everyone is trying to glamorize having a huge number of Instagram followers, but having 10K, 100K or even a million followers means nothing if people are not listening to your message or buying the products/services you are trying to sell.

Aim to have an engaged target audience. For a small local business or startup, getting even 10–15 new customers in a month via Instagram is huge.

On Instagram, if you are trying to

- grow your audience
- generate qualified leads, or
- acquire paying customers,

then this book is right for you.

If you are trying to just get millions of followers without doing the work, then you will have to look somewhere else. Honestly if you focus on getting 1000 true Instagram fans at a time, then eventually you will reach 10K, 100K, or a million followers.

In the email marketing world, having 1000 engaged audience in a list generates huge revenue. And if someone buys 10K mailing addresses, then they may not generate a single dollar. You know why?

Because people buy from people they know and trust.

1

In the last few months, we have done a lot of research on Instagram marketing. We have identified things that work and things that don't. In this book, we have compiled our learnings and research.

This is a short book with actionable strategy and suggested tools without any fluff.

We have created a 3-day Instagram challenge which will help you in getting started with growing your account. You can join that at *http://bit.ly/Friendlyinstagram*

Lastly, I am sure there will be many things which can be added or improved in this book. It would be great if you would provide your suggestions or feedback at *http://www.friendlyagentbot.com/book*

Why Instagram?

Have you tried using Instagram marketing for your business? With more than 1 billion users engaging with Instagram every month, this is one of the best platforms to find your customers. Out of these 1 billion users, around 71% of users are below the age of 35. Hence, whether you are a startup or local business (like insurance agency, real estate agent) or a big company, you cannot ignore Instagram when it comes to marketing.

Remember, a lot of people are visual. As a result, they connect to images they see as opposed to things they read. Therefore, Instagram gives you an opportunity to entice people into wanting to learn more about what you provide in a different way from other social media sites.

Even if you use other online selling techniques, you definitely want to take advantage of Instagram marketing. As one of the highest-ranking social media platforms, this site is a highly effective vehicle for reaching both prospects and existing customers. If you have not yet begun to post photos and videos, you are missing an excellent opportunity.

How I Got Started

It all started with a Facebook post . . .

One day, I saw that my friend has liked a post which mentioned about an insurtech idea-generation workshop happening in Hartford. It was organized by Insurtech Hartford, and since I am from insurance and technology background, I thought I should check it out.

There we were asked to talk about our idea and then teams were formed to brainstorm on those ideas. I talked about chatbot and how it can help insurance companies save money and improve customer service. Out of the few people who joined my group, one was Wade Eyerly, who is a serial entrepreneur. He talked about new startups like Lemonade Insurance who are using chatbot, and we brainstorm about this idea.

Once this event was done, we were told that next event will be a two-day hackathon, so I thought why not give it a try. They had mentors at hackathon who helped in refining ideas and at the end of it, I had a pitch deck and prototype of a product. I thought that this idea will help insurance agencies a lot as they need this to succeed in today's environment.

Next I connected with some of the folks I met at hackathon and who were from an insurance agency background. I was able to convince one of them to give it a try, and this helped me in refining the product and testing it out. The next month, I was able to sign up one or two more agencies, and then it started to look like something that had potential.

I used to do blogging before starting this venture, and SEO (search engine optimization) was one of my strengths. Hence I started a website and start publishing articles regarding chatbots and how they can help insurance players. This helped in getting the next set of customers, who found us online and had similar challenges.

I believe that using the right digital marketing techniques combined with chatbot can help insurance players grow exponentially.

We also got a chance to be part of accelerator called reSET in Hartford, and there we learned a lot and met some amazing folks who still continue to support and motivate us.

I have talked to hundreds of insurance agents/insurtech startups and continue to learn from their experiences and challenges.

One challenge I keep hearing is that businesses are finding it hard to generate leads. Getting eyeballs to their product and services is their biggest concern. In our business, we are able to address this challenge by using SEO (search engine optimization). But SEO takes time and skills, usually 3–6 months to start getting some kinds of results.

Our clients required something which they can adopt easily to grow their business. I started experimenting on different things like Facebook ads, Pinterest, and finally Instagram. And Instagram clicked.

To our surprise, within a month, we started getting new leads via Instagram.

I started experimenting with different techniques to generate followers/leads via Instagram and documenting those results. Then I thought, *why not share my learnings with others* and hence this book.

One thing which I noticed is that 95% of websites hardly get any traffic and 5% are getting most of the traffic. Our chatbots are good for people who are generating tons of traffic and looking for ways to convert that traffic to a paying customer. We ourselves have sold chatbots using our chatbot.

Through this book, I am trying to help those 95% of the audience that is struggling to get traffic and generate leads in a sustainable fashion.

Getting Started: Initial Setup

Convert to Instagram Business Profile

If you are currently having a personal profile, then you should convert it into a business profile ASAP.

Keep in mind that a business profile has several different capabilities compared to a personal profile. Therefore, you want to pay close attention to the details when setting up your account.

The business profile also provides you analytics regarding your Instagram account, which will in turn help you in identifying what is working and what's not.

It will provide you metrics like the number of people visiting your profile, number of website clicks, number of views of your post, demography of your audience, and much more.

How To Set Up An Instagram Business Profile

Select a high-quality profile picture that stands out and grabs attention. Also, you need a professionally written bio so potential customers can immediately see the value that your business offers.

In the name field, you should add information about the services you offer. For example, you can mention " Real estate agent" or "Marketing Expert" or "insurance agent" rather than mentioning your name.

Pro Tip: Create your bio in a notepad and then copy it in your Instagram bio. It is difficult to edit in Instagram, and this will allow you to add spaces and emojis easily. Don't forget to add hashtags relevant to your business. If you are an insurance agent, add #insuranceagent in your bio.

How to Gain Followers on Instagram

Hashtags: Key to Growth

Do not forget to use hashtags. With those, you can group your Instagram posts while leveraging current trends on social media. You also can create a hashtag for your business.

Something else to consider is that because you can search for updates on any given topic, hashtags make it easier for people to find your business, which helps generate followers and likes.

Instagram allows 30 hashtags per post. As a rule of thumb, you should have 10 hashtags that are focused toward your customers/product with more than a million posts; the next 10 should be between 500K to million posts; the last 10 hashtags should be super focused with a smaller number of posts like 50K to 250K.

Once you are done curating hashtags relevant for your business, you should keep them in a notepad or Evernote. This will help in copying and pasting them easily on your Instagram posts.

Pro Tip: Instead of stuffing all the hashtags in your post, you should put them in the comment section. Once you have published your post, add a comment, and paste all your hashtags there.

Content Strategy for Instagram

What to Post on Instagram

When posting on Instagram, be sure to post things that people find interesting. As mentioned, this social media platform boosts business through visual content, so it is imperative that you post compelling graphics, photos, and videos. As an example, if you have office staff, include photos of them. If your business recently had a team-building event or volunteered to help a charitable organization, include photos or videos of that as well. You can even use relevant GIFs, memes, and quotes to bolster your success.

Motivational Quotes

Publishing motivational quotes is the easiest way to grow and engage the audience. Who doesn't like a good motivational quote? When you post using hashtags in your niche, you are sure to get a lot of likes and followers.

Q&A

Most people who want to learn about or purchase your product will have a lot of questions. Use your Instagram account to provide answers to key questions through a series of short videos.

Emotion

Regardless of the content you post, the goal is to evoke emotion. The best ways to accomplish this is by posting the photos and videos that create a connection between your followers and your business. A picture of that cute dog in your office is sure to connect you with your dog-lover audience.

Humor

Although selling your product or services is serious business, it is important for you to show your human side using humor. Never feel nervous about giving your followers a peek at your personality. The goal is to find a balance of addressing an important topic and having a little bit of fun. Developing a human connection will go a long way in helping your agency succeed. By doing this, people will see you as approachable, honest, and authentic.

Instagram Content Calendar

Come up with an Instagram content calendar based on these categories and upon analyzing the competition.

You can use tools like Buffer to schedule your posts in advance so that you are not scrambling every day for a new post.

You can use an app called Phonto to edit your image and add text content. You can also add other images and your logo using this tool.

Instagram Competitor Analysis

Find the top 10 profiles in the subject area/niche in which you are trying to grow. Analyze what kind of posts are getting the most engagement in terms of likes and comments. Come up with an Instagram content calendar based on this analysis.

Follow folks who are commenting and liking your competitors' posts. Also try to engage with them. These are going to be the most engaged audience whenever you post something.

You can find your competitors by searching top posts for a hashtag.

Engage With Your Audience on Instagram

If someone is commenting on your post, then you should respond to them. Similarly, you should find posts that are relevant to your business and leave a comment.

Instagram tracks engagement metrics, and the more engagement you get on your post in first 15–30 minutes, the more reach you will get.

If you notice the account mentioned below, then you will observe that though follower count is only 759, but there are around 505 Instagram users visiting this profile. This high engagement converts to followers website visitors and leads.

Get Instagram Followers for Local Business

If you are a local business such as an insurance agency, restaurant, real estate agent, etc., then you should target based on geography.

Go to the search bar and type your city name. You will find people and tags associated with your city. For example, here we are looking for hashtags related to the city of Hartford.

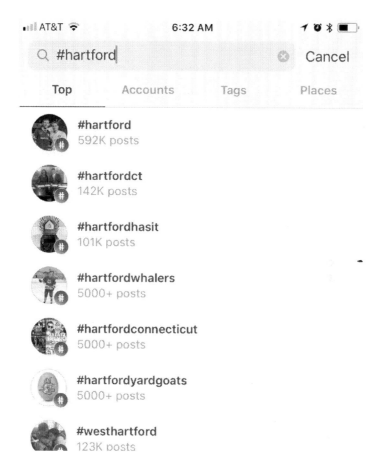

Select the top tag related to your city. You will see all the posts being shared related to the city you want to target. Now go to the "Recent" section, and start engaging with those posts. Most of the folks get 1–2 comments on their post, and if you engage with them, you will start getting their attention. Do this on a daily basis, and you will grow your Instagram exponentially.

Similarly, if you are operating in a particular niche, then you should search for that term (instead of the city) and engage with posts related to the niche.

Instagram SEO

In Google, everyone wants to be on the first page for keywords related to their business. Sites that are on the first page of Google get most of the traffic, and remaining sites hardly get any traffic for those search terms. In Google, the best way to rank is by targeting keywords that are low in competition and relevant to your business.

Similarly, on Instagram, your aim should be to land on the top spot for hashtags your prospects are interested in. Based on the popularity of that hashtag, your post may or may not be visible to your prospects. Hence you should target hashtags which have less competition and are relevant to the topic or your target audience.

You can find the popularity of a hashtag by searching it and finding out the number of posts associated with that hashtag. For example, for #motivation you will find about 200 million posts, and it is difficult to land on the explore page of your target audience, but for #motivationalquoteoftheday, there are approximately 200K posts, and it is much easier to rank for that hashtag.

Instagram Engagement Groups

There are a huge number of people posting on Instagram every minute. You will see a few of those posts on your explore page, and many you will never see.

Instagram measures engagement for a post based on the number of likes and comments. A post with a high amount of engagement lands on top of Instagram's explore page of your target audience. Also, you should be getting high engagement within the first 30 minutes after you publish your post.

One way to get high engagement is by using Instagram engagement groups or Instagram PODS as some are called.

There are two types of Engagement groups:

1) Groups on messaging platforms

There are groups which you can join on Telegram (messaging app) where each member likes/comment posts of other members. Each group is managed in a different way. In some groups, people post on a regular time frame/interval, and everyone will like or comment during that time. Some groups are open, and you can post anytime.

For example, once you publish your Instagram post, you can go to these engagement groups and provide a link to your post. You will start getting likes/comments, and this will boost the rank of your post on Instagram. This, in turn, will give more visibility to other users organically and get more followers/prospects for your business.

2) DM (direct messaging groups) on Instagram

There are certain groups that are formed on Instagram direct messaging and are generally limited to 15 members or fewer. I don't like this method personally as it will get you max 15 likes/comments.

How To Find Engagement Groups

One way is to direct message a profile that has a high number of followers in your niche and ask them if they are part of any group.

You can also form your own group, but it's better to join with people who have a high number of followers.

Join Facebook groups related to Instagram and ask about Instagram engagement groups. We have created a FB group called "Friendly Instagram marketing,"
(*https://www.facebook.com/groups/2335628516524472/*) which you can join.

Collaborate and Grow

Collaborating with other Instagram profiles in your niche is a good way to grow your Instagram. You can have an arrangement where you share their content on your profile and they share yours. This way, you will get exposure to other audiences and gain new followers/prospects.

There are some large accounts that charge to publish content. It makes sense to pay some of these accounts to gain an initial set of followers.

Hacking Techniques—Software for growth

By now you know that in order to grow your Instagram account, you need to share posts regularly, engage with other profiles, and follow and like accounts in your niche.

You can automate some of these processes by using tools and software available online.

Buffer.com

You can use this to schedule your posts in advance so that you are not typing/creating posts every day. You can batch process your posts every week, and this will make sure that you are posting consistently.

Stimsocial.com

This software can follow people who are interested in accounts similar to yours. It will also like posts appearing on your timeline. Software will provide growth in an automated fashion. This coupled with your other efforts can grow your account exponentially.

How to Build a Brand Using Instagram

By definition, branding is a type of marketing strategy that entails creating a name, design, or symbol that makes your business easily identifiable. Overall, this sets you apart from the competition. With branding, people can quickly and easily identify one company from another.

Dozens of brands have built their business on Instagram. Mvmtwatches is one such example. They have built a multimillion-dollar business using Instagram and their marketing channel.

If you look at personal brands, then you will see marking gurus like Gary Vee having huge engaged followings on Instagram.

Every day when you see posts from business or personal brands, you start feeling connected with them. You start developing trust and likeability.

Eventually when Gary Vee launches a new book or MVMT come up with a new watch or promotion, then their fans will line up to buy their products. You should aim to do the same for your business. Big question is how? Let us try to help you with same.

Logo

Your logo serves as a powerful branding strategy for your insurance agency. Take Nike and Adidas as prime examples. Each chose to brand their products with a distinct design. Nike's shoes and apparel have a black swoosh that resembles a wing in the air, which comes from the Greek Goddess of Victory. On the other hand, Adidas opted for a design in the shape of a mountain that represents the various challenges faced by athletes. Although completely different visually, people immediately know one brand from the other.

You have the same opportunity for your business. The right logo will make a lasting impression on both prospects and existing customers, setting the tone for what they can expect when buying products or services from you. Simply put, the brand becomes a true representation of what your business is and how you want people to perceive it.

When it comes to branding, the one thing you should invest in is your company's logo. If possible, work with a professional graphic designer or someone with the skills to use your ideas to create a strong branding statement. If you need to stick to a budget, there are several excellent tools available online. Remember, not only does your logo need to represent your current business but also what you anticipate it becoming in the future.

Make sure to add your logo and brand name while posting on Instagram wherever possible. Try to be consistent with your approach, and post items that are consistent with your brand.

Unless you are a big brand, you should have your real photo on a profile instead of a logo.

Tagline

Because the tagline portrays a specific message, you want to choose something that grabs the attention of and resonates with your target audience. Although a tagline is short, there are many ways to make it powerful and memorable. Look at Nike's tagline: "Just Do It." Those three words provide an impactful message. When having your logo designed or designing it yourself, be sure to integrate your tagline.

Other Intangible Components

Branding goes far beyond logo and tagline. It's what you or your business stands for—your core values, beliefs, and much more.

For example, if your business uses recyclable materials then you should mention same in your posts and use corresponding hashtags. This will attract people who share same belief system as you.

Benefits of Branding on Instagram

Builds Recognition

Branding your business builds recognition. While all the components mentioned play a critical role, your logo and messaging are perhaps the most vital. As with the example provided, you want a logo that is both memorable and powerful. Select something that people quickly recognize, and then include the logo in your posts, in quotes, as part of promotional material, and in your bio.

In case of a personal brand, you should post your picture instead of logo. When we see someone's picture on our Instagram profile daily, we start recognizing them. When you meet that person in the real world, you feel that you know them forever. Even though I have never met Gary Vee in person, I feel that I know a lot about him via his Instagram account.

Makes Marketing Consistent

The more consistent you are in displaying your business's logo or your personality, the more successful you are in your branding efforts. Although it takes time for people to recognize your brand, displaying your logo and your picture (in case of personal brand) wherever you can will speed up the process.

Creates Loyalty

The more that people recognize your brand, the more they'll trust you and your business. Part of that entails providing excellent product and outstanding customer support. For the recognition aspect of branding to turn into loyalty, people have to know that what you offer is of superior value.

Loyalty is often passed down from generation to generation. That means your long-term customers will share they experiences they have with your business, prompting future generations to buy products from you instead of somewhere else.

People stand in line to buy the new iPhone because they are loyal to that brand.

Maximizes Product Launches

If you currently sell one or two types of products/services but plan to expand your offering, brand equity will maximize that effort. With brand recognition, people will pay attention when you announce a new product or service. With the right branding, you encourage people to buy from you or add an existing product to what they already have.

Enhances Credibility

Branding will also make you appear credible. When you combine innovative marketing strategies, outstanding customer support, and fascinating visuals, your business's credibility increases within the industry and among your customers.

Generating Leads via Instagram

Marketing Funnel

Converting unknown entities into customers is the entirety of a marketing funnel. A **marketing funnel for your business** is nothing but a conversion mechanism—*from prospects to the paying clients*.

What you mustn't forget is that you must create measurable value for your potential clientele before you expect to engage them.

The thing about a **marketing funnel** is that without a doubt the leads keep decreasing with every step. That's why it's called a funnel, *isn't it?* There could be multiple reasons for leads to not move forward, but understanding those reasons and improving your marketing funnel is important. So your best bet is to lay out a bigger marketing net to reel in more leads than usual and convert most of the right-fit prospects to customers.

Marketing Campaigns

In order to get people into your marketing funnel, you will need marketing campaigns/strategy. It could be free trials, ebooks, giveaways, referrals, etc., but the trick is to pick one and test it.

Awareness

Once a prospective customer responds to your marketing campaign, the next step is to make them familiar with your brand, business, and in some cases, you. You can achieve this via long form Instagram posts, video, blog posts, ebooks, video tutorials, testimonials, etc.

Acquisition

In this step, you try to get their contact details (email, phone number, social media connection, etc.) by offering them something valuable like a webinar, strategy session, guide, whitepaper, etc.

Qualifying leads is an interesting process, and it could be the first or second stage of your funnel. You can achieve this by asking certain questions when they are trying to sign up for your lead magnet. This will help you in determining whether they are the right fit to pursue further or not.

Once you have a medium to reach out to customers, you can start nurturing those leads via email campaigns and messenger marketing. To ensure a sale, one needs to have the best offer on the table, deliver better content, and arouse of the need of one's product in the minds of the buyer.

Activation

This stage comprises queries related to price, product, and deals offered by the company. To essentially convert a potential buyer to an actual client, this stage must go through smoothly. To avoid a last-minute dropout, you could turn this into a possible conversion by making the client a deal he can't refuse. Leads converting to sales are a marketer's fruit.

Retention

Happy customers refer others, hence it's important that you make it easier for customer to connect with you if needed. Try to get their feedback and determine if they are satisfied or not. You can also ask then for referrals and get new folks into your funnel.

Measure and Improve Your Marketing Funnel

Once you have established marketing funnel, you need to monitor conversion. This will help you in identifying leaks so that you can fix them on time and not burn your leads.

For example, if lot of people are coming to your website but not signing up for your lead magnet, then either you should change the marketing campaign to attract the right customers or change what you are offering as a lead magnet.

How To Get Website Traffic Using Instagram

In your Instagram posts, you are not allowed to add any links to your website, so generating traffic is a bit tough compared to other social media platforms.

The only place where you can place a link is in your bio. Whenever you post something on Instagram, make sure you ask your audience to visit your bio. For example, if your post is related to "5 ways to save on auto insurance," you can mention in the post something like "please visit our bio @yourhandle to get a free guide." This way you are sending people from your post to your bio and then from your bio to your website.

Use Tools Like Linktree

Instagram allows you to have only one link in your bio, but sometimes you may want to have multiple links for different purposes/audiences. You can use tools like "Linktree" to achieve this functionality. Basically, when someone clicks on a Linktree link in your bio, it opens a page which shows multiple links to your audience.

Have a Lead Magnet on Your Instagram Bio

A lead magnet is an offer where you ask some to provide their email address or any other information in exchange for some free valuable resource. If you visit our Instagram page, you will find the lead magnet " 5 ways to generate leads via chatbot."

Once you are able to get an email address from your Instagram audience, you can engage them by providing valuable content via email.

Direct Messaging for Lead Generation

Effective use of direct messaging (DM) on Instagram is key to generating leads and prospects. This does not mean that you start pitching your product in your first message.

Imagine that a guy (say Bob) sends a direct message to someone (say Marry), and that first message says, "Marry Me." How will that go? Probably Mary will flag him, and Bob will not be able to send any further messages.

Best way to start engagement is by offering something of value to prospects for free. It could be a lead magnet like an ebook, webinar, or quiz.

Once prospects sign up for your lead magnet, you can engage with them via email or messenger marketing.

Numbers Game: If you send a direct message to 10 people, then few of them (say 2–3) will sign up, and then some of them will end up as a customers. The more people you engage with, the better your results will be. Finally, it's a numbers game. Someone who can send DMs consistently will gain more customers compared to someone who sends none.

How to Generate a Lead in 7 Days

Day 1: Identify 10–15 Instagram profiles who are your potential customers. You can do this by looking at certain hashtags. For example, we look at #insuranceagent to find insurance agents who can buy our chatbot.

Day 2: Follow these 10–15 profiles and like few of their images, and leave meaningful comments. If it is someone's birthday, then wish them a happy birthday.

Day 3: Again go to these profiles and leave comments and like their pictures. If they receive only few comments on their profile, then they will notice you, and some of them will like and comment on your pictures.

Day 4: Make sure you respond to people who commented on your profile. Send a direct message to them offering some kind of *free* lead magnet. For example, we will message a link for "Five ways to generate leads via chatbot."

Day 5: Again like and comment on their pictures. By now most of them know you, and some will visit your profile to see what you do. Make sure you have updated your bio and mentioned how you can help them. For example, if you provide insurance for high-net-worth individuals, then it should be specified clearly in your bio. Some of them may call you, some will visit your website, and some may send email.

Day 6: Send a direct message and remind them about your lead magnet. Some of them will sign up and enter your email marketing funnel. Keep liking and commenting on their pictures.

Day 7: By now you would have generated few leads either via lead magnet or direct communication from your prospects. You can now move to make a sale. If you sell online, then share a link with a special limited offer. If you sell over the phone, then request an appointment. Keep doing this every week, and you will start getting consistent leads via Instagram.

Instagram Ads

Due to the way Instagram functions, you can target your advertising based on specific traits, including age group, interests, and gender. One critical note: The same company runs both Instagram and Facebook. Unfortunately, you cannot get the same level of details on Instagram users as you can on Facebook users. For optimal results with Instagram ads for your business, link this account with your Facebook account.

Are Instagram ads successful? The answer to this question is a resounding *yes*. For that reason, companies of all sizes and industries rely on this platform, including those involved with insurance. As long as you do everything right, which includes targeting the right audience, you can easily run a campaign for six to eight weeks and increase the number of your followers by the thousands.

There are two ways to run Instagram ads. One is from your Instagram app and other is via Facebook Business Manager. Below we have mentioned how you can run Instagram ads from the app.

When you are running ads from Facebook Business Manager, the process is same as when you run Facebook ads. You can easily find these steps online, so we have not discussed them here.

Step 1: Convert your account to the business profile.

If you are using personal profile for Instagram, then it's time to move to a business account. The steps are simple, and you get added benefits like the ability to view insights/analytics on your posts. You will also be able to run ads via your business profile.

Step 2: Hit Promote on the profile page.

Once you have a business profile, you will see the "Promote" option in your profile. You can hit this button if you want to configure an ad from Instagram itself. The other option is to use Facebook Ad Manager and create an Instagram ad using the account linked with your Instagram.

Step 3: Select the post you are trying to promote.

Now you can select the post you are trying to promote.

Pro Tip: Publish multiple versions of posts on your profile, and check which are performing well. Use for your ad the one that is performing best and getting the most interaction.

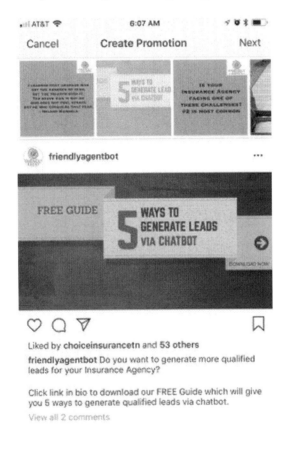

Step 4: Select where you want to send people.

You can select where people should go from your ad. You can send them to your profile, website, or storefront.

Step 5: Select the target audience.

Here you can either target people you are following you or you can create a custom audience.

Step 6: Select the budget.

Next you can select how much you are willing to spend on your ads. You can select a daily limit and the number of days your ad should run.

Step 7: Hit Start Promotion

Metrics Related to Instagram Marketing

Unless you keep track of the right metrics, you will never know whether your efforts related to Instagram marketing are resulting in any real growth or not.

Also keeping track on metrics will help in understanding what is working and what's not so that you can iterate and improve.

Once you convert your Instagram account from personal to business, you get access to analytics/insights.

Some of the metrics you should be tracking are mentioned below.

Follower Growth

If people are liking what you are posting on Instagram, then they will follow you and engage with your content. Having a good number of followers also provides social proof to your business.

Profile Visits

This tells you the number of folks who visited your bio/profile. If you are not getting enough profile visits, then you should add/update a call to action on your post. People visiting your profile will learn more about you and your business.

Website Visitors

Your bio should have a compelling lead magnet to drive people to your website or any other webpage you want them to visit.

Number of Email Subscribers

You should be collecting email addresses of people visiting your website. This will help you in engaging with your prospects via email marketing.

Instagram Marketing Agency

If you have limited time and bandwidth to engage and grow your Instagram account for marketing, then it is a good idea to hire someone to do that for you. We at Friendly Agent also provide Instagram marketing services and can help you in generating leads and growing your business via Instagram. Setup your free strategy call to learn more about how Instagram can work for you.

Website: https://www.friendlyagentbot.com

Conclusion

Instagram marketing done right is one of the most powerful mechanisms to engage customers, generate leads, and grow business.

There are no shortcuts to success, but one can accelerate the process by using a well-defined strategy.

We have created a 3-day Instagram challenge that will help you in getting started with growing your account. You can join that at *http://bit.ly/Friendlyinstagram*

Please feel free to connect with us on Instagram @friendlyagentbot